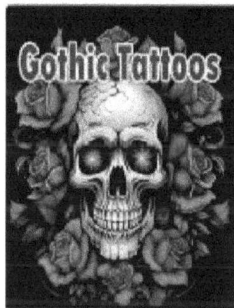

This Notebook Belongs To

_____

_____

_____

SureShot Books

PUBLISHING LLC

Books have the power to change lives.

SureShot Books Publishing LLC is part of the SureShot 2k family of companies that was founded in 1990 to help inmates & their families by making it possible to improve their lives with the Power of Reading.

Here at SureShot Books, we fervently believe that the fact that you have made a mistake does and should not mean that your life is ruined forever.

We believe that everyone deserves a second chance.

Contact Us with any questions or concerns:
SureShot Books Publishing LLC
P.O. Box 924, Nyack, New York 10960
845.675.7505
Email Us:
info@sureshotbooks.com

BIBLE VERSES

Inspirational
Bible Scriptures

COLORING BOOK

BIBLE VERSES
SCRIPTURE FOR ADULTS AND TEENS

Embark on a soulful journey with our 'Bible Verses Coloring Book' tailored for adults and teens. Immerse yourself in the calming embrace of intricate designs paired with uplifting scriptures. This unique coloring experience goes beyond art, offering a pathway to reflection and spiritual connection. Let the pages come alive with your creativity as you breathe life into sacred verses, finding serenity in each stroke. Whether you seek relaxation or a deeper bond with faith, this coloring book is a sanctuary of mindfulness, inviting you to explore the intersection of art and spirituality. Rediscover the joy of coloring with purpose.

FEAR NOT
isaiah
41:10

GIVE THANKS to the LORD FOR HE IS GOOD

The CHEERFUL heart  HAS A CONTINUAL FEAST

 Proverbs 15:15

MY GRACE is all YOU NEED MY POWER works best in WEAKNESS

2 corinthians 12:9

ACT justly LOVE mercy WALK humbly MICAH 6:8

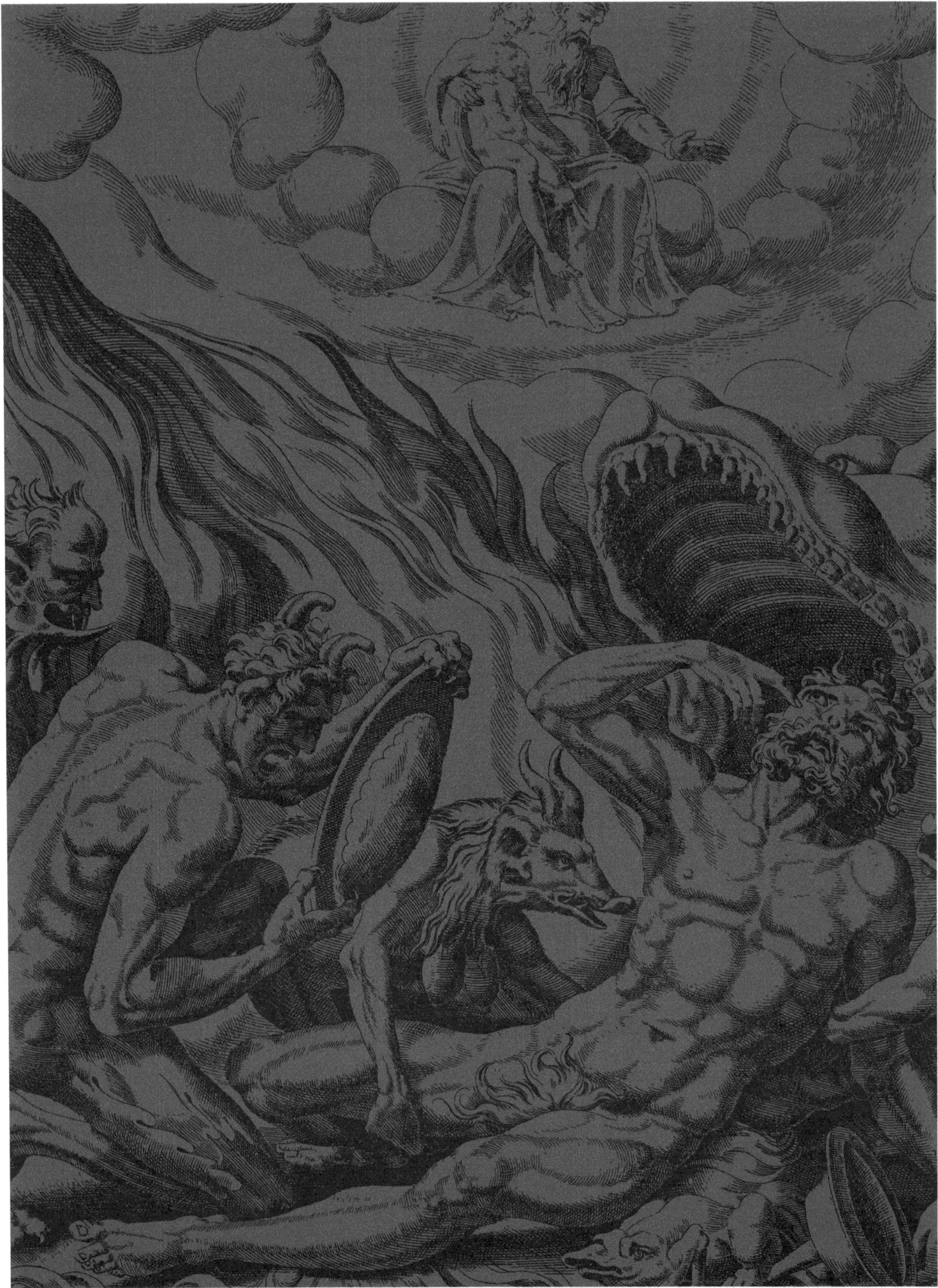

Be still
AND KNOW
that i am
GOD
PSALM 46:10

BE
strong
and
courageous
JOSHUA 1:9

MADE TO WORSHIP

PSALM 95:1

SEEK
Peace
AND PURSUE IT.
PSALM 34:14

RISE up and PRAY

TAKE
Heart
I HAVE OVERCOME THE
WORLD
JOHN 16:33

Anchor
of the soul
Hebrews 6-19

Beautiful covered girl

Psalm 91:4

Believe in the light

John 12-36

Fear Not

ISAIAH

41:10

Free indeed

JOHN 8:36

i know who holds tomorrow

not perfect + just

FORGIVEN

1 JOHN 1:9

Faith over Fear

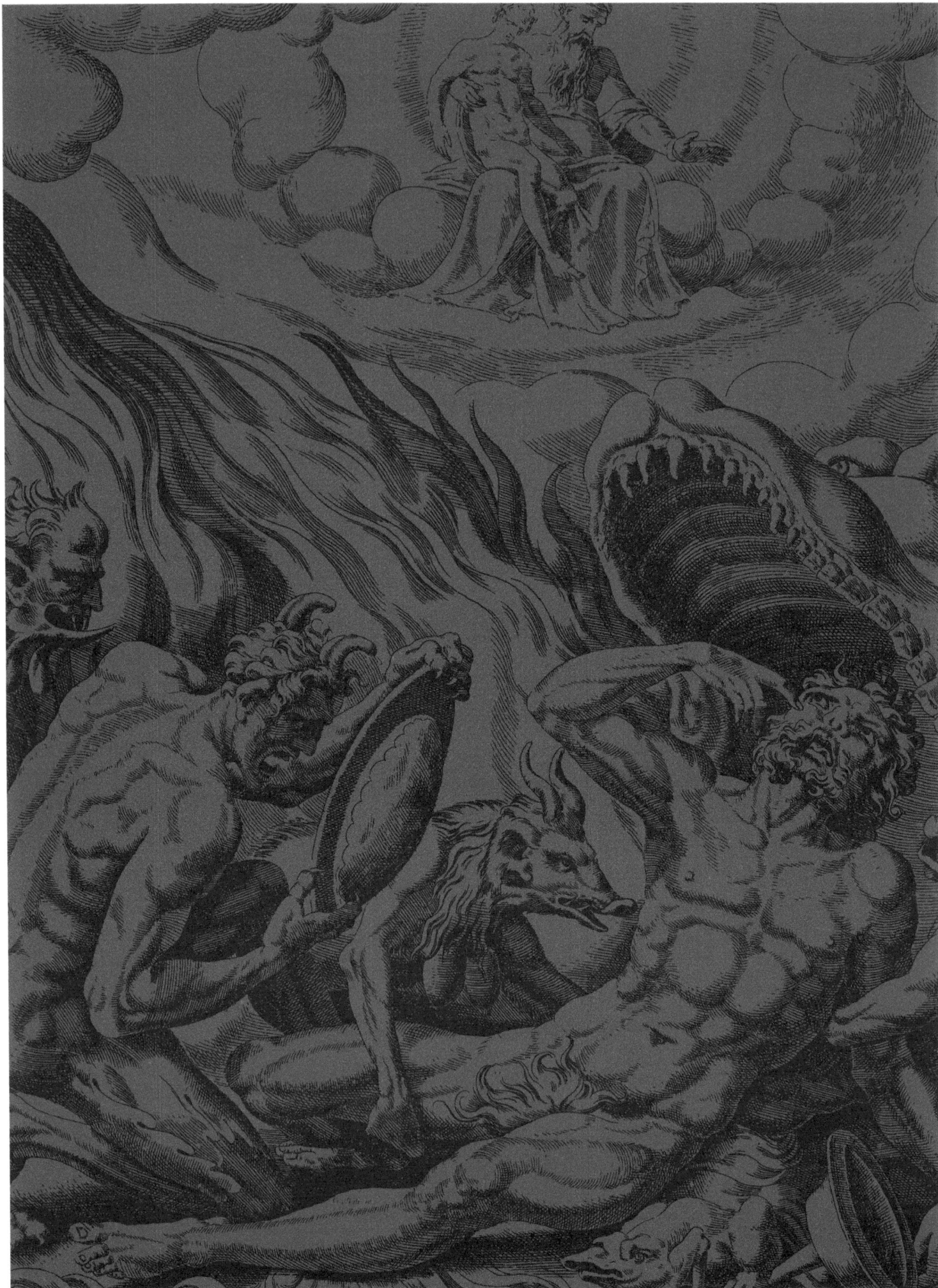

Jesus † ⊙ † loves ♡ me ♡

BE THE + light

MATTHEW 5:14

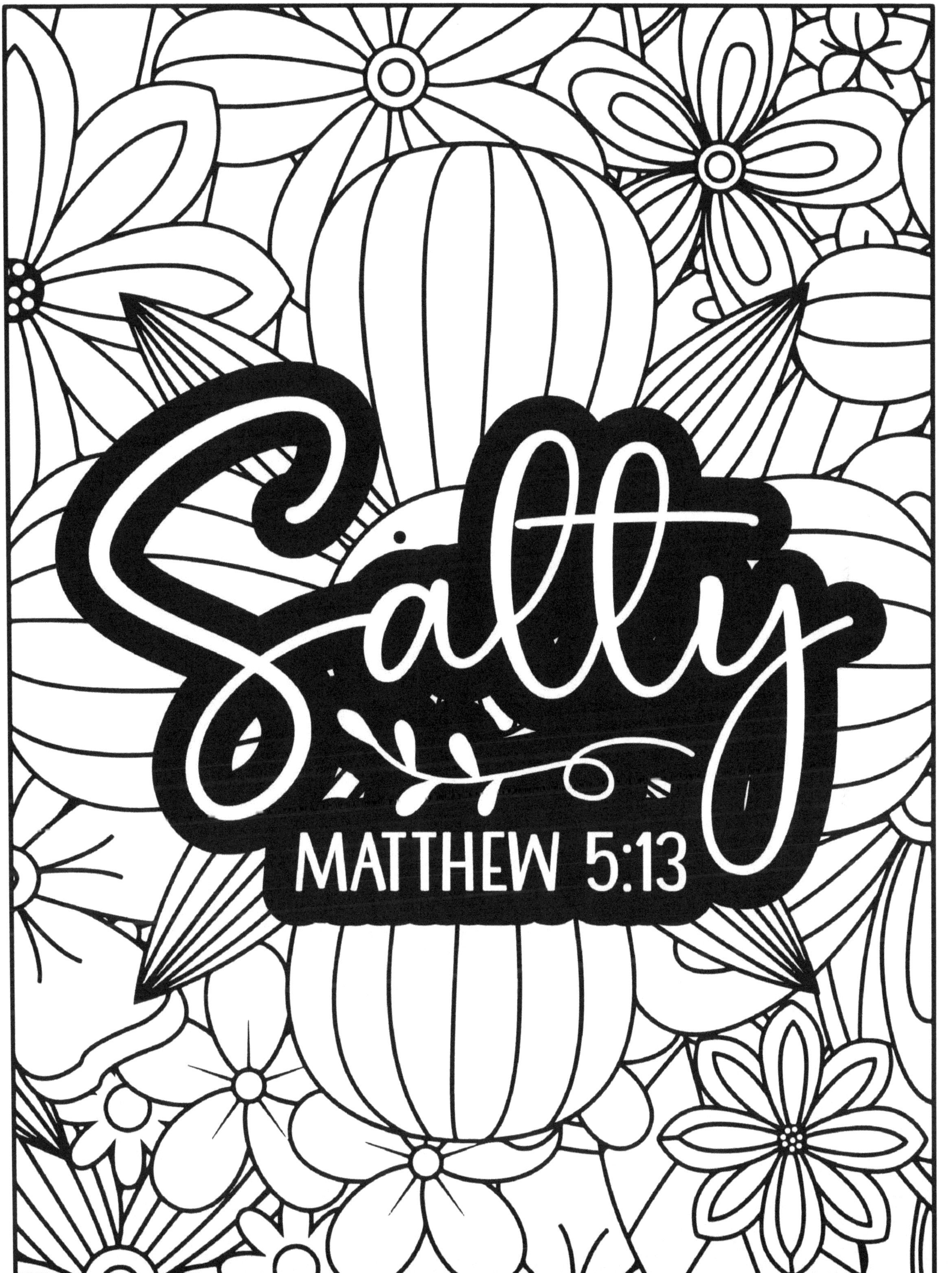
Salty
MATTHEW 5:13

SHE IS Strong

PROVERBS 31:25

BE Still my soul

She Laughs Without Fear of the Future

Proverbs 31:25

Choose JOY

Romans 15:13

FORGIVEN, Redeemed, LOVED

A man's heart deviseth HIS WAY but the lord DIRECTETH HIS STEPS

PROVERBS 16-9

ACT *Justly* LOVE *mercy walk* HUMBLY

micah 6:8

And when i WAKE UP YOU ARE STILL with me Psalm 139:18

Arise
for it is your
TASK
and
WE ARE
with you
BE STRONG
and do it

Be still and KNOW THAT i am GOD Psalm 46:10

Be on your GUARD STAND FIRM IN THE FAITH BE COURAGEOUS be strong

1 corinthians 16:13

Be strong AND Courageous
JOSHUA 1:9

Bless the food BEFORE US THE FAMILY BESIDE US and The Love Between Us

Cast all *your* **ANXIETY** ON HIM Because He Cares For you 1 PETER 5:7

GOD IS faithful ALL THE time

SHE IS far MORE than RUBIES

god is
faithful
all the
time

MORE FAITH less fear

WHEN YOU GO THROUGH DEEP WATERS I WILL BE WITH YOU

A family is God's masterpiece

Bless our Home

Created with a purpose

Raise a hallelujah

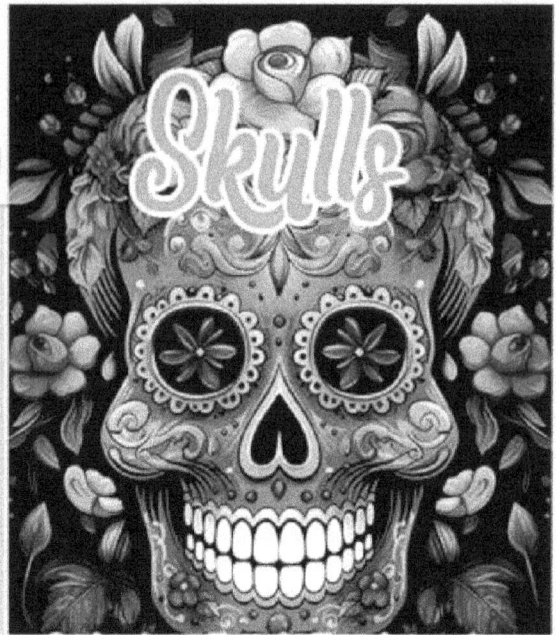